To
André
from Boo (ya bird)
16.05.03

Machines

Written by Colin Hynson
Illustrated by Mike Atkinson

p

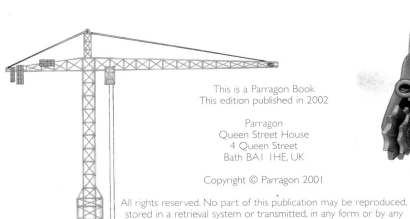

This is a Parragon Book
This edition published in 2002

Parragon
Queen Street House
4 Queen Street
Bath BA1 1HE, UK

Hardback: ISBN 0-75256-954-6
Paperback: ISBN 0-75257-068-4

Printed in China

Produced by
Monkey Puzzle Media Ltd
Gissing's Farm
Fressingfield
Suffolk IP21 5SH
UK

Cover design: Design Principals

Contents

4 Machines for Building
6 Machines for Digging
8 Machines on the Farm
10 Machines in the Home
12 Health
14 Communication
16 Music
18 Entertainment
20 Machines at Sea
22 Machines on Land
24 Machines in the Air
26 Machines in Space
28 War Machines
30 Machines of the Future
32 Index

How is liquid concrete delivered to the top of a building?

When a building is being constructed, the steel frame is built first. Liquid concrete is then poured into it to create floors and walls. A pump uses compressed air to force the concrete up a pipe so that it can be delivered at the required height.

How fast is a paver?

A paver is used to lay down a layer of hot tarmac on the surface of a road. This is a very slow process, and the paver moves at less than 1 kph (0.65 mph) as it performs its work.

Why doesn't a crane fall over?

Near the top of the crane's vertical tower, there are two horizontal arms, or "jibs". One is much longer than the other. The longer jib is used to lift heavy objects. The shorter, "counterweight" jib has large concrete blocks built into it. These balance the weight on the main jib and prevent the crane toppling over.

How do builders stop concrete hardening?

Concrete will set and harden very quickly unless it is kept moving. So builders keep it in a concrete-mixer. The large barrel of the mixer revolves constantly, and the curved, metal blades inside it stir the concrete and prevent it setting.

What is a machine?

A MACHINE IS A PIECE OF APPARATUS WITH several different parts – each with its own function – which uses the energy put into it to produce and direct force. People use machines to make different tasks possible or easier. Vehicles, tools, weapons and musical instruments are all types of machine. A simple bicycle and a sophisticated satellite are both machines. In the building industry, machines range from basic pulleys to complex bulldozers, cranes, drills and dump trucks.

Why don't skyscrapers fall over?

Because skyscrapers are so tall, they need deep foundations to prevent them toppling over. At the foot of a skyscraper, builders drive steel girders called piles into the ground and set them in concrete. To hammer the piles in, they use a machine called a pile-driver, which is basically a very heavy weight on the end of a crane.

The world's largest truck – the Terex Titan.

How is air used to drill?

A PNEUMATIC DRILL IS POWERED BY AIR. THE AIR IS PUT UNDER pressure by a compressor, then fed to the drill through a rubber pipe. When the trigger of the drill is pressed, the compressed air is pushed into a cylinder just above the drill's blade or "bit". This forces the bit downwards into the ground. Almost immediately, the air is released into another cylinder which pushes the bit back up. This all happens several times a second.

What is the Terex Titan?

The Terex Titan 33-19 built by General Motors is the world's largest dump truck. It is nearly 17 m (56 ft) long, and with a full load it weighs 549 tonnes. Its fuel tank can hold 5,909 litres (1,300 gallons) of diesel.

Did moles dig the Channel Tunnel?

THE CHANNEL TUNNEL IS REALLY THREE TUNNELS. TWO OF THEM ARE USED BY trains and a smaller tunnel is used for maintenance and repairs. The tunnels were built using giant tunnelling machines called "moles". The moles, which are the same width as the tunnels they dig, hollowed out the earth with powerful spinning blades. They were guided by laser beams linked to satellites, so they could follow their planned route to the nearest metre.

How does an excavator move its arm?

Excavators have a mechanical arm, which is called a hydraulic ram. The arm is made up of a piston inside a cylinder. There are reservoirs of fluid at the top and bottom of the cylinder connected to it with pipes. The fluid is pumped through either pipe at high pressure, which moves the piston up and down and controls the arm.

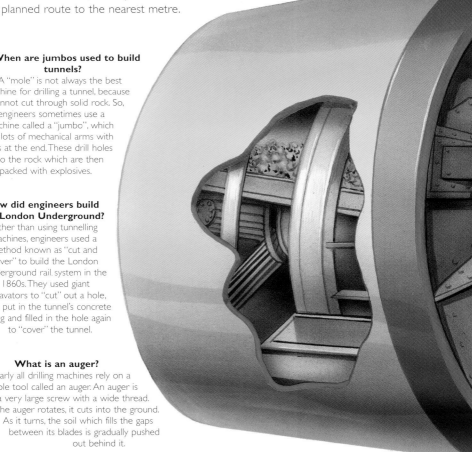

A laser-guided tunnel-boring machine, or "mole".

When are jumbos used to build tunnels?

A "mole" is not always the best machine for drilling a tunnel, because it cannot cut through solid rock. So, engineers sometimes use a machine called a "jumbo", which has lots of mechanical arms with drills at the end. These drill holes into the rock which are then packed with explosives.

How did engineers build the London Underground?

Rather than using tunnelling machines, engineers used a method known as "cut and cover" to build the London Underground rail system in the 1860s. They used giant excavators to "cut" out a hole, then put in the tunnel's concrete lining and filled in the hole again to "cover" the tunnel.

What is an auger?

Nearly all drilling machines rely on a simple tool called an auger. An auger is just a very large screw with a wide thread. As the auger rotates, it cuts into the ground. As it turns, the soil which fills the gaps between its blades is gradually pushed out behind it.

Why are diamonds used for drilling?

When drilling for oil and gas, a drill has to bore through some very hard rocks. The metal teeth that spin round and cut into the rock are tipped with diamonds, because diamond is the world's hardest material.

What was Orukter Amphibolos?

Machines called dredgers clear routes for boats by dragging a bucket along the bottom of a waterway. Horse-powered dredgers have been around for over 500 years, but the first steam-powered machine was built by Oliver Evans in 1804. He called it Orukter Amphibolos which means "amphibious digger".

Diamond-tipped drillbits like this are used to bore through solid rock.

What is Big Muskie?

It is not always necessary to dig tunnels for mining.

Many mines are simply very large holes in the ground, where digging machines called excavators are used to scoop out precious rocks and minerals. Machines called "drag-line" excavators use a giant bucket on the end of a cable to haul up rocks. Big Muskie, which does its work in Ohio, USA, is the biggest of all drag-line excavators. It weighs over 12,000 tonnes, and is the largest vehicle of any kind.

7

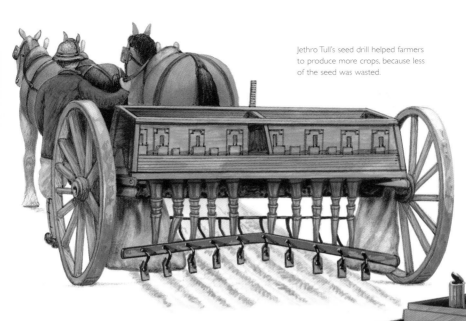

Jethro Tull's seed drill helped farmers to produce more crops, because less of the seed was wasted.

What did Jethro Tull invent?

JETHRO TULL INVENTED THE FIRST MECHANICAL SEED-DRILL.

Before his invention people sowed seeds by scattering them by hand. Tull's machine could plant several rows of seeds at regular intervals, which meant that less seed was wasted. Tull built his first seed-drill in 1701, and used it on his own farm without telling anybody else for thirty years. His invention was the first step in the use of machines in British agriculture.

How do farmers use aircraft?

In some parts of the world, farmers have such large fields that they use aircraft to spray their crops with insecticides. These kill anything that might damage the plants. Crop-spraying is not as popular as it used to be, because of environmental damage.

Is a tractor as strong as a horse?

Tractors can actually have the same pulling power as 200 horses. Most of the machines on a farm could not operate without them. A tractor's powerful engine pulls ploughs, muck-spreaders and mowers.

How old is the plough?

Paintings in ancient Egyptian tombs show ploughs drawn by oxen. These prove that the plough has been used as a machine for at least 5,500 years. But machines change and develop. The first plough entirely made of iron was designed in Norfolk, England, by Robert Ransome in 1785.

What machines make hay?

Many farmers grow fields of grass called forage to feed their animals in winter. They use a special mower to cut this grass, which is squeezed between two rollers to get rid of water. The grass dries in the sun and becomes hay. It is then gathered up by a machine called a baler, which packs the hay into a tight bundle called a bale.

How does a farmer fertilize a field?

Manure from farm animals feeds the soil, helping plants to grow. Farmers use machines called "muck-spreaders" to spread the manure. They are pulled by tractors, and contain chains which revolve quickly and fling out manure in all directions.

How did a mathematician in ancient Greece help farmers?

ARCHIMEDES, WHO LIVED IN THE THIRD CENTURY BC, INVENTED the Archimedes Screw which has been used by farmers for over 2,000 years. It is a large wooden screw inside a wooden case. The bottom of the screw is put into water. A handle is turned, and the rotation of the screw draws water up to the top to be used for watering crops.

Archimedes also discovered laws about two other important machines – the lever and the pulley.

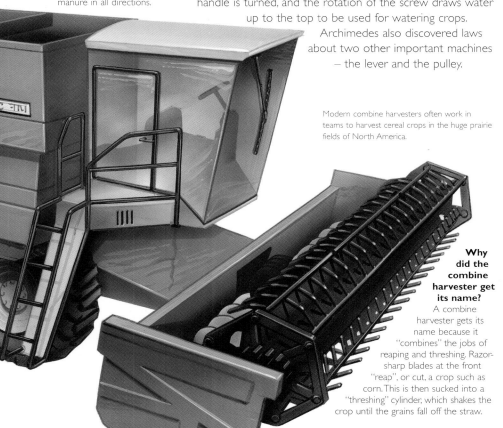

Modern combine harvesters often work in teams to harvest cereal crops in the huge prairie fields of North America.

Why did the combine harvester get its name?

A combine harvester gets its name because it "combines" the jobs of reaping and threshing. Razor-sharp blades at the front "reap", or cut, a crop such as corn. This is then sucked into a "threshing" cylinder, which shakes the crop until the grains fall off the straw.

9

How did vacuum cleaners hoover before Hoover?

One of the first portable electric cleaners was developed by James Murray Spangler in 1906, who sold his rights to the machine to William Henry Hoover. Before this, vacuum cleaners were powered by hand pumps!

A modern vacuum cleaner.

How do refrigerators make food cold?

A REFRIGERATOR WORKS BY REMOVING HEAT FROM THE FOOD. A LIQUID called a refrigerant is pumped into a coil of pipes near the ice-box called the evaporator. Pressure is used to make this liquid evaporate. As a liquid evaporates, it reduces temperature. So, the refrigerant becomes colder. When a hot object comes into contact with a cold object, its temperature is lowered. So, as the refrigerant becomes colder, so does the food.

What essential household machine did Queen Elizabeth I's godson invent?

In 1596 Elizabeth I's godson, the writer Sir John Harington, published the first design for a water closet – a toilet with a water-filled cistern that could be flushed by removing a plug. He recommended that it was flushed at least twice a week.

Why do washing machines have concrete inside them?

Washing machines need a lot of weight inside them to cut down the vibrations caused when the drum is spinning at full speed. Without that weight the washing machine would be very unstable and would wander about the room.

How do heaters know when to turn themselves on and off?

Heaters have a thermostat, which contains two strips of metal joined together. When the temperature increases, the two metals expand by different amounts and make the strip bend. This bending turns the heater off. When the room cools, the strip straightens and turns the heater back on.

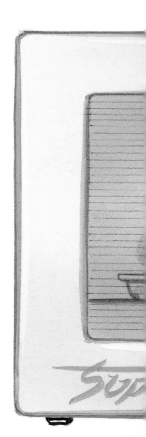

How do microwave ovens make food hot?

Microwave ovens produce radio-waves, which are scattered evenly throughout the oven by a small fan. These waves pass easily through paper and glass and most kinds of china. But when they enter food, they create a magnetic field which causes the water molecules in the food to vibrate at 2.5 billion times every second. This vibration causes friction, which creates heat, which cooks the food.

When were light bulbs first created?

During the 1840s there were many attempts to create a light bulb, but the filaments inside the bulb did not last long enough to make them worthwhile. In 1879 the American inventor Thomas Edison developed the first successful bulb using a filament made from carbon.

How do TV remote controls work?

Remote controls use infra-red, which is a light-wave our eyes cannot see. The remote control sends out an infra-red signal to a sensor on the television called a photo-diode, which translates it into an electrical signal. This signal changes the channel.

The microwave oven was invented in 1945, but the first ones did not go on sale until 1967.

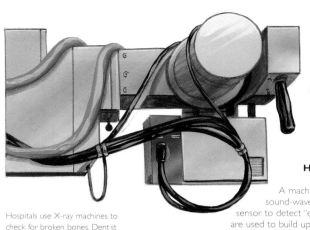

How does an X-ray machine work?

X-rays are electromagnetic waves similar to light. X-rays can easily move through the skin of a patient but they are absorbed by bones and teeth. They are beamed through a patient's body on to photographic film, where the shadows of bones show up any fractures.

Hospitals use X-ray machines to check for broken bones. Dentist often use them too, to detect areas of decay in teeth.

How can sounds look inside a patient's body?

A machine called an ultrasound scanner sends sound-waves into the patient's body, and uses a sensor to detect "echoes" of these sounds. These echoes are used to build up a picture on a screen. Ultrasounds are often used to look at an unborn baby.

What machines look after babies?

New-born babies can be placed in machines called incubators, which provide an ideal environment for a baby's health. The amount of oxygen, warmth and humidity can all be regulated in an incubator, and germs can be kept out.

What does MRI mean?

MRI stands for Magnetic Resonance Imaging. We are all filled with tiny biological magnets, and MRI uses these natural magnets to build up a picture of the inside of a patient's body. It is safer than an X-ray which produce radiation that is harmful in large amounts.

What is a sphygmomanometer?

A SPHYGMOMANOMETER IS A MACHINE USED TO READ BLOOD PRESSURE. IT HAS an inflatable cuff, a pump, and a gauge filled with mercury. A nurse wraps the cuff around the patient's upper arm and uses the pump to inflate the cuff until it is tight enough to stop the blood flowing to the lower arm. Air is then released until the blood flows again, at which point a pressure reading can be taken from the gauge.

How can a CAT help you in hospital?

DOCTORS USE A CAT (COMPUTERIZED AXIAL TOMOGRAPHY) SCAN TO build up a three-dimensional "map" of a patient's body. The patient lies on a table inside a circular scanning machine, and X-rays are passed through their body from many different angles. Computers then convert the readings into a detailed picture. CAT scans can detect such things as tumours and blood clots.

How does a respirator work?
Patients who have lost the use of muscles required for breathing can be placed inside a respirator. The air pressure inside the respirator is decreased causing the patient's chest to rise, which draws air into the lungs. The air pressure is then returned to normal and the chest falls, forcing out the air.

What is an endoscope?
Doctors use an endoscope to look inside a patient's body. The endoscope is a long, thin tube containing two bundles of fibre-optic cables. It is inserted into the body, and light is bounced along one bundle. This light is reflected back along the other bundle, creating a detailed image of the tissue.

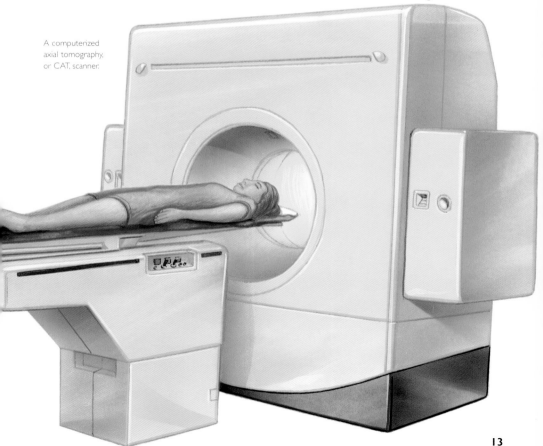

A computerized axial tomography, or CAT, scanner.

How did the Cold War create the Internet?

DURING THE 1960S, THE US MILITARY WERE LOOKING for ways to protect information on computers in the event of a nuclear attack. In 1969 they started the ARPAnet project, which linked all the computers in the US Defence Department around the country. This ARPAnet network eventually grew into the world-wide network of computers we know as the Internet.

All around the world, hundreds of millions of people use the Internet for work, education and leisure.

Who was the first criminal to get caught by radio?

In 1910, Dr Harley Crippen murdered his wife and tried to escape to Canada with his mistress. A description of Crippen was transmitted to the ship by radio, and the captain recognized him among his passengers. He radioed the Canadian police who were waiting when the ship arrived.

How do mobile telephones communicate?

Mobile telephones are actually radio transmitters and receivers. A cellular phone network is divided into geographical areas known as cells. Inside each cell is an antenna that keeps track of all mobile telephones in that cell. When one is dialled, the call is sent to its last known location. If it is not there, then neighbouring cells are checked.

Was the telegraph a British or American invention?

It was a British invention, but the American version became more popular. In 1837, the British inventors Charles Wheatstone and William Cooke invented the five-needle telegraph. In 1841, Samuel Morse first demonstrated his own system, which used the famous "dot and dash" code.

How does a fax machine work?

When a document is fed into a fax machine, a scanner divides the picture into tiny black or white squares called pels. These are sent down the telephone line as a series of electrical signals. A black pel means the signal is on, a white pel means it is off. These electric signals can be used to reconstruct and print the original picture.

When was the first telegraph cable laid under the Atlantic?

The first Atlantic cable was laid in August 1858, but by September a fault had developed. In July 1866, the ship *Great Eastern* set off from England to the USA and successfully connected the two countries with nearly 4,500 km (2,800 mi) of cable.

Which radio needs no electricity to work?

In 1991, Trevor Baylis invented the clockwork radio. This wonderful machine enables people without a supply of electricity to listen to radio programmes. Over 20,000 a month are made in a factory in South Africa.

Who invented the telephone?

THE AMERICAN ALEXANDER GRAHAM BELL invented the first working telephone. The telegraph, a machine which could transmit sounds, had already been invented, but Bell's was the first machine to transmit speech. Bell applied for a patent for his new invention in 1876. Another inventor, Elisha Gray, applied for a similar patent for his own invention only two hours later. If only he could have phoned!

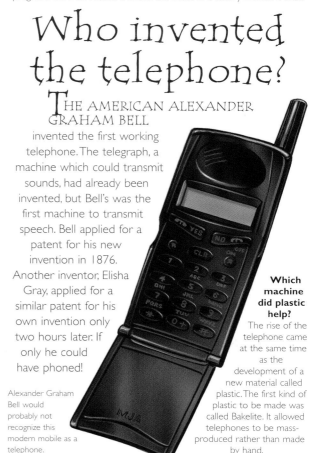

Alexander Graham Bell would probably not recognize this modern mobile as a telephone.

Which machine did plastic help?

The rise of the telephone came at the same time as the development of a new material called plastic. The first kind of plastic to be made was called Bakelite. It allowed telephones to be mass-produced rather than made by hand.

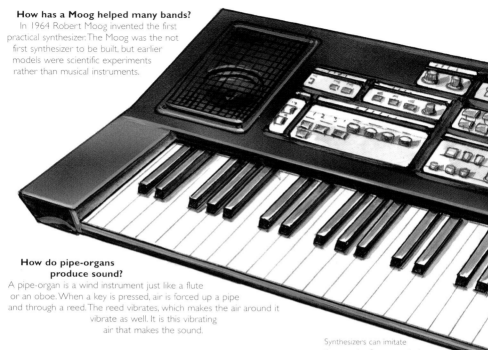

How has a Moog helped many bands?

In 1964 Robert Moog invented the first practical synthesizer. The Moog was the not first synthesizer to be built, but earlier models were scientific experiments rather than musical instruments.

How do pipe-organs produce sound?

A pipe-organ is a wind instrument just like a flute or an oboe. When a key is pressed, air is forced up a pipe and through a reed. The reed vibrates, which makes the air around it vibrate as well. It is this vibrating air that makes the sound.

Synthesizers can imitate the sounds of many musical instruments, and can also create totally new sounds.

What machine can a musician use to keep time?

MUSICIANS CAN TRAIN THEMSELVES TO KEEP THE RIGHT TEMPO, OR time, by using a machine called a metronome. This was invented in 1812 by the Dutchman Dietrich Winkel. It has an upside-down pendulum that swings back and forth in regular time. A weight can be moved up and down the pendulum to adjust the speed. Modern metronomes are electronic. They are more accurate and keep time with either a noise or a light.

How old is the piano?

Keyboard instruments like the harpsichord have existed for many centuries, but they could not play notes at different volumes. The piano, or pianoforte, solved this problem. It is believed that the first piano was built by the Italian Bartolommeo Cristofori in about 1709. He called it a "harpsichord that plays soft and loud".

How do the Chinese classify their musical instruments?

The Chinese divide their instruments into eight classes, depending on the material that creates the music. The classes are metal (bells), stone (chimes), silk (stringed instruments), bamboo (flutes), wood (percussion), skin (drums), gourd (windbox) and clay (pipes).

What musical machines run on clockwork?

Music boxes run on clockwork. When they are wound up, a barrel with metal pins begins to revolve. These pins then pluck the teeth of a steel comb. The length of each tooth determines the pitch of the note.

What was the "Frying Pan"?

The Frying Pan was the name given to one of the first electric guitars, built in 1932. It had been developed by Adolphus Rickenbacker, a Swiss toolmaker who had settled in Los Angeles, USA.

Plucking the strings of an electric guitar makes very little sound, unless the guitar is connected to an amplifier and loudspeaker.

How is a theremin played?

THE THEREMIN IS UNIQUE AMONG MUSICAL MACHINES BECAUSE the player does not need to touch it at all. The theremin sends out radio-waves which can be moved about by waving both hands around the instrument. These changes are picked up by an antenna and translated into different sounds. The theremin was invented in 1920, and was used successfully by the Beach Boys in 1966 on their hit single *Good Vibrations*.

A mini hi-fi system comprising a CD player, cassette deck and radio connected to stereo loudspeakers.

How can a laser beam listen to music?

The surface of a compact disc or CD is made up of a spiral track containing billions of microscopic pits. A CD player shines a laser beam through the plastic on the bottom of the CD. The beam is reflected back by the CD's metal coating. The variations in this reflection, caused by the pits, are translated into sound by a microprocessor.

Where could people listen to the first juke-box?

The first juke-box was installed in the Palais Royal Saloon, San Francisco, USA, in 1889. But people were not allowed to make their own music selections! The first proper juke-box, where people could choose a song, arrived in 1915.

When was the first personal stereo made?

Personal stereos were introduced in 1979 by the Sony Corporation. They called them "Walkman boogie-paks". Sony have since sold over 100 million of their little machines.

What is a television picture?

If YOU LOOK CLOSELY AT A TELEVISION SCREEN, YOU WILL SEE THAT IT contains hundreds of horizontal lines. Each of these lines contains hundreds of different-coloured dots. From a distance, these dots merge together to create the illusion of a complete picture. A television screen is only capable of showing three colours, red, green and blue. These colours merge with each other to create all the different colours on the screen.

What was the first successful computer game?

In 1971, Nolan Bushell designed Computer Space. Using the small profits from this game, Bushell constructed Pong for Atari, which was the first commercially successful arcade game.

How does a machine make movies "move"?

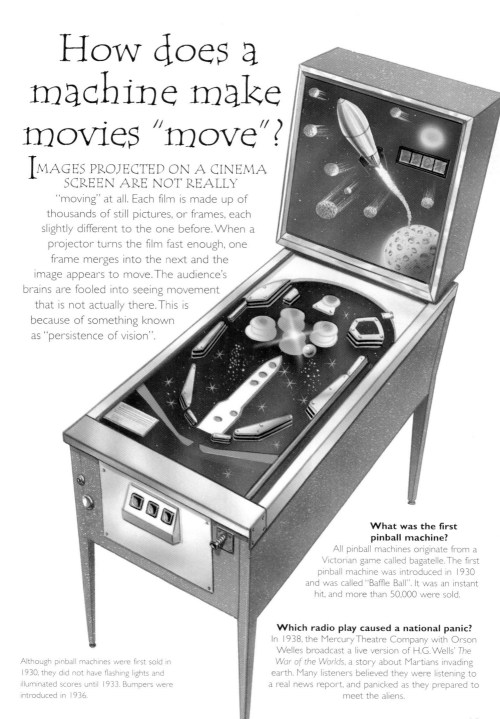

IMAGES PROJECTED ON A CINEMA SCREEN ARE NOT REALLY "moving" at all. Each film is made up of thousands of still pictures, or frames, each slightly different to the one before. When a projector turns the film fast enough, one frame merges into the next and the image appears to move. The audience's brains are fooled into seeing movement that is not actually there. This is because of something known as "persistence of vision".

What was the first pinball machine?

All pinball machines originate from a Victorian game called bagatelle. The first pinball machine was introduced in 1930 and was called "Baffle Ball". It was an instant hit, and more than 50,000 were sold.

Which radio play caused a national panic?

In 1938, the Mercury Theatre Company with Orson Welles broadcast a live version of H.G. Wells' *The War of the Worlds*, a story about Martians invading earth. Many listeners believed they were listening to a real news report, and panicked as they prepared to meet the aliens.

Although pinball machines were first sold in 1930, they did not have flashing lights and illuminated scores until 1933. Bumpers were introduced in 1936.

19

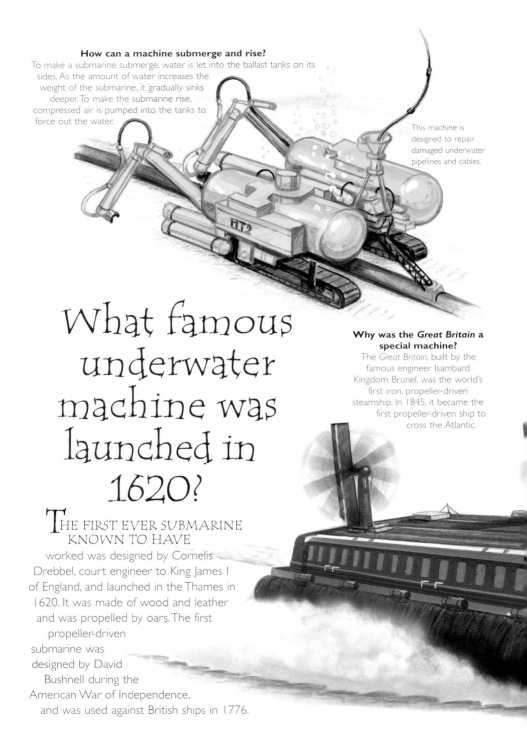

How can a machine submerge and rise?

To make a submarine submerge, water is let into the ballast tanks on its sides. As the amount of water increases the weight of the submarine, it gradually sinks deeper. To make the submarine rise, compressed air is pumped into the tanks to force out the water.

This machine is designed to repair damaged underwater pipelines and cables.

What famous underwater machine was launched in 1620?

Why was the *Great Britain* a special machine?

The *Great Britain*, built by the famous engineer Isambard Kingdom Brunel, was the world's first iron, propeller-driven steamship. In 1845, it became the first propeller-driven ship to cross the Atlantic.

THE FIRST EVER SUBMARINE KNOWN TO HAVE worked was designed by Cornelis Drebbel, court engineer to King James I of England, and launched in the Thames in 1620. It was made of wood and leather and was propelled by oars. The first propeller-driven submarine was designed by David Bushnell during the American War of Independence, and was used against British ships in 1776.

When did a submarine first travel under the North Pole?

In 1958, the USS *Nautilus*, the world's first nuclear-powered submarine, became the first submarine to travel under the North Pole without surfacing. It took 96 hours to travel the 2,946 km (1,830 mi) under the ice.

What machines are good at breaking the ice?

Ships called ice-breakers are used to cut channels through frozen seas. These powerful machines either batter through the ice with their reinforced bows, or ride up on the ice and break it beneath their own weight.

How deep can machines dive?

Machines called submersibles have extremely strong hulls to withstand water pressure, so they can descend to incredible depths. In 1960, a submersible called *Trieste* dived down almost 11 km (7 mi) below the surface of the Pacific.

What are the world's biggest ships?

The world's biggest ships are enormous oil tankers called supertankers. The biggest is the *Jahre Viking*, which is over 458 m (1,500 ft) long. It was almost completely destroyed during the Iran-Iraq war, but was rebuilt and launched again in November 1991.

An oil tanker

How does a hovercraft work?

Hovercraft are also called air-cushion vehicles, because they are supported on a cushion of air up to 2.5 m (8.25 ft) deep. Large fans on a hovercraft suck in air and force it downwards, where it is contained by a flexible skirt. Floating on this cushion of air, and driven by propellers, a hovercraft can travel over land or water. The fastest hovercraft can reach 105 kph (65 mph).

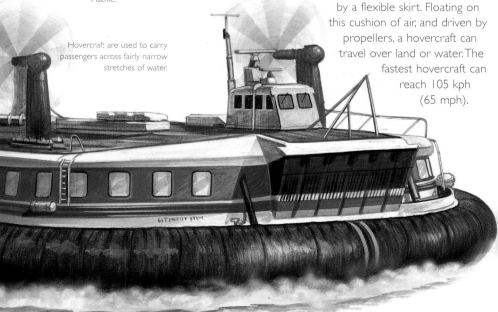

Hovercraft are used to carry passengers across fairly narrow stretches of water.

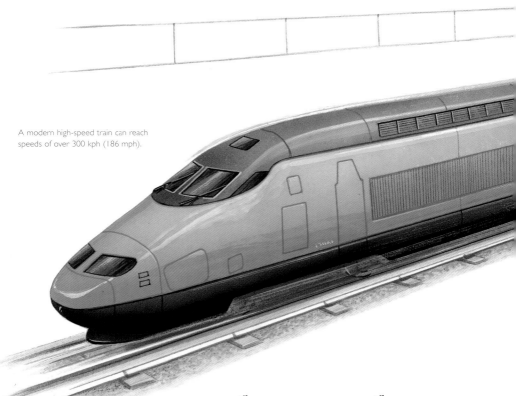

A modern high-speed train can reach speeds of over 300 kph (186 mph).

Who invented the train?

The first steam-powered vehicle that ran on rails was built by the English engineer Richard Trevithick. He demonstrated it on Christmas Eve 1801, by pulling some passengers up a hill. In 1808, Trevithick built a circular track in Eaton Square in London, and charged people to travel in a carriage pulled by a train.

What was the longest freight train in the world?

In August 1989, a freight train made a journey of 861 km (535 mi) through South Africa. It was made up of 16 locomotives and 660 wagons. The combined length of the locomotives and wagons was 7.3 km (4.5 mi).

What machine joined the east and the west of the USA?

IN JANUARY 1863, 10,000 WORKERS BEGAN LAYING RAILWAY TRACK WESTWARDS from Sacramento. In December 1865, 12,000 workers started a track eastwards from Omaha. The two lines eventually met at Promontory Point, Utah. The last two pieces of track were joined together with a gold spike on 10 May 1869. It was now possible to take the train from the Atlantic to the Pacific coast of America.

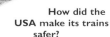

The USA was the first country to put lamps on the fronts of its trains. At first, these were piles of burning wood in iron baskets, but by the time of the American Civil War, most trains had oil-lamps with powerful reflectors to throw the light forward.

What kind of machine was the Tin Lizzie?

TIN LIZZIE WAS THE NICKNAME GIVEN TO THE MODEL T FORD, THE MOST

popular early motor car. It was first built in 1908, and was so popular that the Ford Motor Company introduced the first ever "assembly line" of workers to build it. By 1919, half of all the cars in the entire world were Model Ts. Production ceased on 31 May 1927, when number 15,007,003 rolled off the assembly line.

Why did Nicolas Cugnot's machines get him arrested?

In 1769, the French military engineer Nicolas Cugnot built one of the first vehicles powered by a steam-engine. The weight of the huge copper boiler at the front made the machine difficult to steer and it crashed into a brick wall. His second vehicle turned over, and Cugnot was arrested as a public nuisance.

Where does a tram get its power?

On the roof of a tram, there is an arm known as a pantograph. The pantograph connects the tram to overhead cables with a constant electrical current running through them. This current is used to power the tram.

How big are the world's longest and smallest cars?

The largest car in the world has 26 wheels, is over 30 m (98 ft) long, and contains a swimming pool and a king-size water-bed. The smallest car still in production is the Smart car made by Daimler-Benz, which is less than 2.5 m (8 ft) long.

Even a small car like this is a complicated machine, with thousands of working parts.

What famous artist designed a flying machine over 500 years ago?

The ITALIAN ARTIST, GENIUS AND INVENTOR LEONARDO DA Vinci sketched and described a helicopter in 1483! Unfortunately, it would have been impossible for him to build his flying machine because he did not have a lightweight power source. Leonardo wrote down the secret notes of his inventions in a code which could only be read with the help of a mirror.

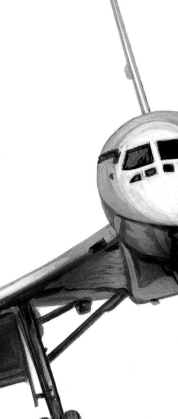

What are the *Bumble Bee Two* and the *Baby Bird*?
The *Bumble Bee Two* is the world's smallest biplane. It was built by Robert Starr and is 2.69 m (9 ft) in length. The *Baby Bird* is the world's smallest monoplane. It was built by Donald Stits and is 3.35 m (11 ft) long.

What did Captain Chuck Yeager break with a machine?
During the 1940s, there were many attempts to fly faster than the speed of sound, but aeroplanes always broke up as they approached supersonic speed. The first plane to finally break through the sound barrier was Captain Chuck Yeager's Bell X-1, on 14 October 1947.

Concorde and other passenger aircraft are powered by huge jet engines.

How does a jet engine obey the law?
A jet engine obeys Sir Isaac Newton's third law of motion, which says that for every action there is an equal and opposite reaction. Air is sucked in at the front of the engine, heated, and pushed out at the back. The opposite reaction to air's movement is the forward thrust of the jet.

Helicopters are often used by armed forces because they are fast and highly manoeuvrable.

How big is the world's largest cargo plane?

The Russian Antonov AN-124 is the largest cargo plane in the world. It can carry over 140 tonnes of cargo in its enormous cargo hold.

Who built the first helicopter?

Leonardo may have thought of it, but the French inventor Louis Breguet got the helicopter off the ground in 1907. His machine hovered just 0.6 m (2 ft) in the air. The first helicopter with just one set of rotating blades, designed by Igor Sikorsky, first flew in May 1940.

Which of the Wright brothers was the first to fly?

How does an ejector seat work?

When an aeroplane is in trouble, its pilot sometimes activates an ejector seat. A powerful gun on the back of the seat fires downwards, and a rocket is fired, causing the pilot and the seat to shoot up to 90 m (295 ft) into the air. A small parachute called a drogue slows down the pilot's descent before the main parachute opens.

ORVILLE WRIGHT FIRST FLEW AT KITTY HAWK, NORTH CAROLINA, ON 17 December 1903. He and his brother Wilbur became interested in powered flight in the late 1890s. They experimented with over 700 flights of kites and gliders to work out how an aeroplane might be controlled in the air. Once they had solved this problem, they built a lightweight engine and propeller, and launched the first successful aeroplane.

How does a machine help astronauts space walk?

WHEN AN ASTRONAUT LEAVES A spacecraft and goes "space walking" he or she can move in zero gravity by wearing a Manned Manoeuvring Unit (MMU). This machine is attached to the back of a spacesuit. It has twenty-four tiny gas jets on it, which can be fired at different times to move the astronaut in any direction. Because each MMU costs about $9 million, only three have ever been built.

What was the largest space rocket?

The American rocket Saturn V dwarfs any other rocket ever built. It flew from 1967 to 1973 as part of the Apollo moon missions. It was 110.6 m (363 ft) high, weighed over 2000 tonnes on the launch pad, and could carry 150 tonnes in space.

An astronaut wearing an MMU during a space walk.

What is a "geostationary" satellite?

Many communication and weather satellites orbit at about 36,000 km (22,370 mi) above the Earth, and travel at the same speed and in the same direction as the Earth. This makes them appear to stand still. Satellites which always remain above the same point on Earth in this way are called "geostationary".

Which planet was the first to be explored by satellite?

The first satellite to fly past another planet was the American *Mariner 2* which passed by Venus on 14 December 1962. The Soviet Union's *Venera 9* landed on Venus thirteen years later and provided close-up photographs of the surface.

Which machines are carrying messages for aliens?

Pioneer and Voyager spacecraft are set to leave our solar system, carrying objects chosen to show life on Earth to any aliens they meet. The Voyagers have a gold-plated record which plays greetings in sixty languages and the sounds of birds and whales.

Where do satellites get their energy from?

Once a satellite is in space it needs electricity to work. This electricity comes from solar cells in large panels on the sides of the satellite. These are pointed at the Sun, and solar energy is converted into electricity and stored in batteries.

What was the first machine in space?

THE FIRST MACHINE IN SPACE WAS *SPUTNIK I* WHICH WAS LAUNCHED BY THE SOVIET Union on 4 October 1957. It was a test satellite and contained a radio beacon and a thermometer. Its launching was a great surprise to many people in the West and marked the start of the "space race" between the USA and the Soviet Union. The second Sputnik was launched one month later and carried the first living thing into space – a dog called Laika.

How does a space shuttle resist heat?

Unlike any spacecraft before it, the space shuttle can be used again and again. When a shuttle re-enters Earth's atmosphere, it is subjected to extreme heat. So, each shuttle is covered with 20,000 silica tiles, made from high-quality sand, which can withstand temperatures of 1,260 °C (2,300 °F).

The outside of each Space Shuttle is covered with thousands of heat-resistant tiles.

What is a "smart bomb"?

Through history most bombs and missiles have been "dumb" – they just fly in the direction in which they are fired. Computers on board modern bombs and missiles make them "smart". They can change course, hunt for targets, and decide whether or not to attack them.

How old is the cannon?

A picture of a cannon appears in an English manuscript of 1326 called *On the Duties of Kings*. It shows a vase-shaped cannon being lit with a red-hot iron, and an arrow flying out of the end.

Huge transporter planes like this are used to carry soldiers and their equipment between military bases.

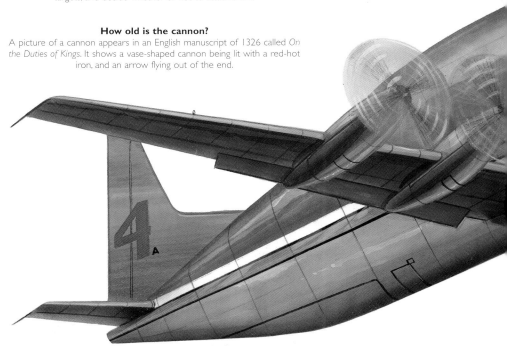

Who invented the machine-gun?

THERE WERE MANY ATTEMPTS TO INVENT A MACHINE THAT WOULD FIRE BULLETS rapidly and without the need to pull the trigger more than once. The first successful machine-gun was designed by Richard J. Gatling in 1862. His "Gatling gun" had a revolving cylinder with ten parallel barrels. It could fire 1,200 shots a minute and was soon used by every major army in the world. An improved, fully automatic machine-gun was patented in 1884 by Sir Hiram Maxim – who also invented the mousetrap!

Which country produced the first guided missile?

During the Second World War, Germany developed two types of guided missile which they used mostly against London and the Belgian city of Antwerp. These terrifying war machines were called the V-1 and V-2, but were known as doodlebugs.

Why do guns "recoil" when they are fired?

They are obeying the same law of physics – every action has an equal and opposite reaction – as jet planes (see page 24). When a bullet leaves the barrel in one direction the gun moves or "recoils" the other way.

Why is a jeep called a jeep?
In 1941, the US government gave motor manufacturers seventy-five days to come up with a new "general purpose" vehicle for the military. The contract was won by Willys-Overland Motors, who built over 600, 000 of the new "jeeps" between 1941 and 1945. The name jeep came from the initials GP – for "general purpose".

What is radar?
Radar stands for radio detection and ranging, and works by sending out radio-waves then measuring how long it takes for them to bounce back. In this way, radar can track objects which are thousands of kilometres away.

How can a war machine become invisible?
The US Air Force's B-2 "stealth" bomber aeroplane has a sleek shape like a wing to deflect radio waves, and is painted with a special coating which absorbs them. So, it is difficult to detect by radar, and becomes "invisible" on a radar screen.

When did the tank become a war machine?

LEONARDO DA VINCI SKETCHED AN IDEA FOR A TANK OVER 500 years ago. But the tank was first used in warfare during the First World War, at the Battle of the Somme in 1916. It was a lozenge shape, and the armour was only about 6 mm (0.25 in) thick so it did not give the crew of eight much protection. During development, the British called their new war machines "water tanks" to conceal their purpose from enemy spies.

An American Abrams M1 battle tank.

How small will machines be in the future?

In ther near future, small hand-held machines may act as a phone, TV, video player, computer and e-mail machine in one.

SCIENTISTS AND ENGINEERS WORKING IN THE FIELD OF "NANOTECHNOLOGY" are looking for ways to make machines as small as possible, so they can work with individual atoms and molecules. Scientists will soon be building machines 100 nanometres in length. That is about the same size as a common cold virus. Tiny nanorobots will one day be sent into the bloodstream to remove or repair damaged tissue in the human body.

Who will do the housework of the future?

Many household machines will become "intelligent", and will be able to communicate with each other and with their owners. Refrigerators will be able to tell when milk supplies are low and order more. Robots can already understand spoken commands, and in the future will do housework without being given instructions.

How will we communicate in the future?

In Britain, the number of people buying a mobile phone is rising by about 10,000 a week. Soon, mobile phones will display video pictures, so that people can look at each other while they speak, and will be able to send and receive e-mail.

Will entertainment change much?

The rise of digital technology means that people will have a much greater choice of television programmes to watch. There will be hundreds more channels to choose from, and viewers will be able to choose their own programmes and decide when to watch them. Football fans can already choose which camera to watch a game from.

What use are virtual reality machines to surgeons?

Surgeons use virtual reality today to help with their training. One day it will help surgeons to perform complex operations even though they are thousands of miles away from the patient. The surgeon will look into a mask which will show the body of the patient, and wear gloves which move a robotic arm over the patient.

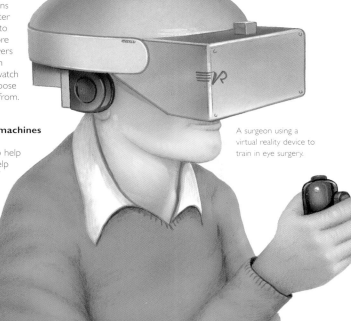

A surgeon using a virtual reality device to train in eye surgery.

How will machines travel in the future?

THE AMOUNT OF OIL AVAILABLE TO POWER THE MANY MACHINES WE use for travel will soon become scarce and run out. Vehicles of the future will have to become very fuel efficient and will need to find new sources of power. These might include hydrogen, alcohol or solar power. Trains of the future might be powered by a high-strength magnetic field. The Japanese are already developing such "maglev" trains.

How will war machines of the future hide themselves?

Scientists are developing the "stealth" technology that makes aircraft invisible to radar. They are trying to make "stealth" submarines, and even "stealth" body-suits that make soldiers and their equipment "disappear".

What is virtual reality?

Virtual reality is a computer-generated, three-dimensional world, which seems real to people using it. It can make computer games very realistic. In the future, people will experience the thrill of dangerous activities such as bungee-jumping without being exposed to any danger. Special suits will imitate the sensation on the skin of wind or water.

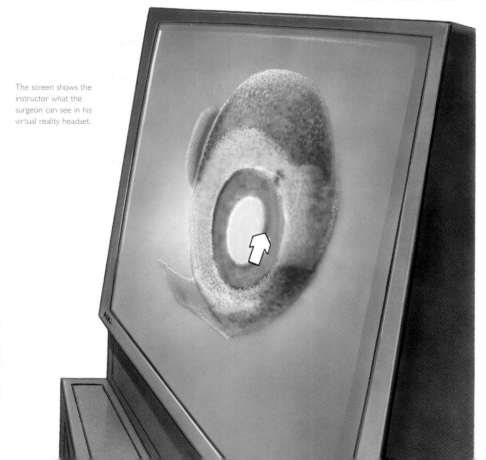

The screen shows the instructor what the surgeon can see in his virtual reality headset.

Index

AB

aeroplanes 24–5, 29
air 24–5
aliens 27
Archimedes Screw 9
astronauts 26
augers 6

balers 9
Big Muskie 7
biplanes 24
blood pressure 12
bombs 28
building 4–5

CDE

cannons 28
cargo planes 25
cars 23
Channel Tunnel 6
cinemas 19
clockwork 15, 17
combine harvesters 9
communication 14–15
compact discs (CDs) 18
computer games 18
concrete 4
cranes 4
crop-spraying 8

diamonds 7
digging 6–7
doodlebugs 28
dredgers 7
drills 5, 7, 8

e-mail 30
ejector seats 25
endoscopes 13
entertainment 18–29
excavators 6, 7

FGH

farming 8–9
fax machines 15
freight trains 22
Frying Pan 17
future 30–1

guitars 17
guns 28

health 12–13
heaters 10
helicopters 24
home 10–11
hovercraft 21
hydraulic rams 6

IJKL

ice-breakers 21
incubators 12
infra-red 11
Internet 14

jeeps 29
juke-boxes 18
jumbos 6

Laika 27
land 22–3
levers 9
light bulbs 11
London Underground 6

MNO

machine-guns 28
metronomes 16
microwave ovens 11
missiles 28
mobile telephones 15, 30
Model T 23
moles 6
monoplanes 24
Morse, Samuel 15
movies 19
muck-spreaders 9
music 16–17

nanotechnology 30

Orukter Amphibolos 7

PQR

pantographs 23
pavers 4
pels 15
personal stereos 18
pianos 16
pinball machines 19
Pioneer 27
pipe-organs 16
planes 25, 28
plastic 15
ploughs 8
pneumatic drills 5
pulleys 9

radar 29, 31
radios 15, 19
refrigerators 10
respirators 13
robots 30
rockets 26

STU

satellites 6, 26, 27
scanners 15
sea 20–1
seed-drills 8
skyscrapers 5
space 26–7
sphygmomanometers 12
Sputnicks 27
steamships 20
submarines 20, 21, 31
submersibles 21
supertankers 21
synthesizers 16

tanks 29
telegraphs 15
telephones 15
Terex Titan 5
theremins 17
thermostats 10
Tin Lizzie 23
tractors 8, 9
trains 22, 23, 31
trams 23
TV 11, 18, 30

ultrasound scanners 12

VWXYZ

vacuum hoovers 10
virtual reality 30, 31
Voyager 27

war 28–9
washing machines 10
water closets 10
Wright brothers 25

X-rays 12